ABOUNDING IN GRACE

Pointing out the way for you to obtain & utilize

Ogar A. VynEdison

Amazon.com

ISBN-979 8558 431 490

Cover design by: Art Painter
Library of Congress Control Number: 2018675309
Printed in the United States of America

INTRODUCTION

ABOUNDING IN GRACE

POINTING OUT THE WAY FOR YOU TO OBTAIN &

UTILIZE!

ABOUNDING IN GRACE IS NOT A PRAYER TOPIC, NEITHER IT IS AN EVENT BUT A REALM (AN EXPERIENCE OF A WAY OF LIFE) TO BE LIVED. IT IS DESIGNED BY GOD AND THOSE WHO THINK AND BEHAVE ACCORDING TO THIS REALM, GOD CALLED THEM PRIESTS ACCORDING TO 1PETER 2:9,10. IT'S A NEW STATUS IN LIFE TO BE WALKED IN, ABOVE THE PERILS OF THIS WORLD, BEING 'ENABLED' TO OPERATE WITH EASE ISAIAH 27:11. A GOOD UNDERSTANDING OF THIS WILL DELIVER RESULTS WITHOUT STRESS PROVERBS 13:15. TO CONTINUE THINKING AN BEHAVING IN COMPLACENT TO DELIGHTING IN GOD YOU BECOME SURROUNDED BY SUCH A DIMENSION OF ITS AROMA THAT AUTO-

MATICALLY COMPELS ACCEPTABILITY EPHESIANS 1:6, IT STRIKES AWE AND WONDER ABOUT YOU AMONG THE NATIONS, DEUTERONOMY 4:5,6. YOU GROW ABOVE CRITICISM INTO PRAISE-WORTHINESS. THE GENERAL PERCEPTION ABOUT YOU CHANGES GALATIANS 2:9. YOUR LANGUAGE GET CHANGED AND SEASONED, EVEN AS HIS WORD RESIDES IN YOUR HEART COLOSSIANS 3:16.

ABOUNDING IN GRACE

Ogar A. VynEdison

ABOUNDING IN GRACE

AN UNDERSTANDING FOR ACCESSING, OBTAINING AND UTILIZING GRACE.

What Is Grace?

Grace is the opposite of karma, which implies getting what you deserves in opposite to Grace, getting what you don't deserve. Grace is the most important concept in the Bible, Christianity, and the world. It is most clearly expressed in the promises of God revealed in Scripture and embodied in Jesus Christ (Justin Holcomb). J. Gresham Machen wrote, "The very center and core of the whole Bible is the doctrine of the grace of God." In studying the subject of Grace and how to secure and utilize it, some points are worth noting which I am hopeful shall help our focus. The subject of grace is as old as man or better put, older than man. Being a factor we all came to meet in existence we have attempted to explain, name, categorize, describe and even argue it. Among a large body of the church it has been held to mean what seems like some kind of un-merited favour that God in all His wisdom selectively pour out upon some, while others are left to their own fate. In supporting this view and concepts they have spent time to backup all such claims with their experiences. Grace is mercy, not merit. Being mercy, we are thus enjoined to come boldly unto the throne that we may obtain. The subject of grace being so deep and broad, man in his limited mental capacity would never fathom all its depth, breath, wideth and length. In any case we have encountered and experienced this grace which have led us to grabble with various definitions, mostly according to our encounters. Our Identity is guaranteed, according to 1 Corinthians 1:10, "By the grace of God I am what I am." Our very existence and life, future, behavior, holiness, strength and sufficiency are all dependent upon this factor-Grace.

THE ROOT OF GRACE

The root word for grace "CHARIS", a Greek transliteration word, definition from G5485; mentioned about 156 times in the Bible, it means enablement and it includes graciousness of manner or act; literal figurative or spiritual; especially the divine influence upon the heart and its reflection in life. Jews in the Hellenistic era, personified this force with a feminine pronoun placing her in the class of goddesses alongside Wisdom {Khokhmah} and others. Being identified as an emanation from YHWH, she is attributed with fruitfulness, results, success etc. It becomes more confusing as we are constantly enabled in various areas of our lives, so we tend to define this grace. In actual sense, we are describing the effects of grace rather than searching for its cause; what it is all about and what its meant for, perhaps its operations and how it is to be accessed, utilized or utilized for our benefits. Grace exist and could be understood in its various forms and applications hence, it remain an all round enabler towards any area of life it is brought upon to bear. One of the major beneficiary who utilized this grace said,

"But by the grace of God I am what I am: and this grace which was bestowed upon me was not in vain; but I laboured more abundantly than they all: yet not I, but the grace of God which

was with me" 1Corinthians 15:10.

It's established herein that through knowledge, grace for outstanding results is specifically sought after with a corresponding action of work from such a seeker. That grace is available and being a free gift, it doesn't just accomplish things for people on its own without the utilizer's imput through work.

* * *

EVEN AUTOMATIC SYSTEMS
ARE A REACTION.

I could liken grace to {PMS} in an engine. Mere pouring in of motor spirit into an engine would not jump start and run that engine but by man's action of turning on the ignition. A man's action is therefore required to set that engine into motion in order to utilize the premium spirit poured into that engine. Unfortunately, many people's understanding of grace is liken to saying, both the premium spirit, igniting of the engine, running and accomplishing the purpose of their engines should just become automatic. This grace is capable of enabling anyone on any venture only if such would give attention to its workings. In this book we shall attempt to underscore and trace the root and source of grace; how it could be secured at will and utilized. In various churches, it has always enthralled many at the dimensions of its working, being preached and witnessed, hearing testimonies of its accomplishments and sometimes we even envy those beneficiaries. We have wished, desired it, even hoped and prayed for it, but it seems to be eluding us and leaving us in delusion of why can't we access this grace that is capable of enabling us achieve our desired results. And in our despair, we have left seeking it perhaps, limited only to now written prayer requests and hoping that most times also that the ministers should pull this grace upon our petitions just to have them fulfilled.

I am imploring you to ingest this book in your hand to really come to an understanding of the factors surrounding this most sought after GIFT of YHWH for our profiting withal. The roots of this great enabler shall be laid bared according to the LIGHT of God at work to help us comprehend and apply ourselves to this truth unveiled herein. Grace is a God factor, which we all have consented to, if so then, it's only wise to get closer perhaps a friendship relationship with God in order to access, secure and utilize it. We are being invited to the source without prequalification required rather open to all:

"come boldly unto the throne of grace..."

What other compelling and rich invitation could we ever seek for, than this? Hence, all that anyone could ever amount to is traceable to this grace, herein you have got an open invitation to partake likewise. Henceforth, we shall no longer be lacking!!

Grace, among a large number of professing Christians, is held in believe to mean an unmerited favor, but favor in itself is just a part of grace, such as acceptance, easy-likeableness and helps etc. Grace exist in various forms which include all of the universal free gifts of life to all of God's creations.

It is in the light of the above we are attempting to present here what are those shrouded factors surrounding this wonderful gift to man-kind and the world. Let us constantly bear in mind that the light of God in regard to any issue of life cannot be fully grasp but we speak according to the level of the revelations of the said light that has infiltrated our souls, being also God's providence and a form of grace. I am not in any better position to explain grace other than an attempt to pen down the light in its little dimension of what is opened unto me.

The points to note

❖ Grace is available

❖ Grace has a custodian

- The custodian dwells in a throne
- We have a responsibility of understanding it
- Grace is a subtle covenant
- The covenantor – God
- The covenantee – Priests (man)
- An invitation is sent forth to partake in it
- Altar of the throne – the meeting point
- God's ultimate aim

The subject of grace under discussion here is a little bias in favour of the church of Jesus and His elects- (priests). We have already said grace is "Charis" enablement. It is divine in nature, being attributed and preceded from God. Inclusive of man, other creations enjoy and flourish by same grace though in various kinds. Many in the church share in the one amongst many possible definitions of grace: that it is an unmerited favor which to most people is usually referred to as luck, this could make grace look like a factor some few fellows are privileged to stumble upon. Some religious people would admonish seekers to first, become born-again after which the said grace should come upon them. Being diverse and many in kinds of this received enablement, men therefore attempt to identify such according to that light e.g, helps, favors, luck, star, anointing, enablement and grace.

* * *

The Delusion

In the quest for this enabling factor to ease our various life journeys, many religious leaders have taken undue advantage in robbing others of their resources with the promise of imparting this grace. Cases abound with both the local as well as the federal authorities of fraudulent practices of these religious leaders. They range from giving and receiving of lands, cars, cash, properties etc in promised exchange of the anticipated graces which nothing actually was gained by such seekers, it become more worrisome as many who have believed in this divine enablement cannot yet access it.

YOU MUST ACKNOWLEDGE IT

From time immemorial, all of God's creations are being made by this factor so much to the extend that even from the pages of the Bible men whom this grace enabled to become whatsoever the height they attained yet refused to acknowledge God as the sole factor for their exploits of greatness, rather arrogate such to themselves or their gods have always ended with the withdrawal of such graces only to their failures and thus incurred the wrath of the divine giver.

The king spake, and said, is not this great Babylon, that I have built for the house of the kingdom by the might of my power, and for the honor of my majesty? While the word was in the king's mouth, there fell a voice from heaven, saying, O king Nebuchadnezzar, to thee it is spoken; The kingdom is departed from thee. Daniel 4:30-31;

But when his heart was lifted up, and his mind hardened in pride, he was deposed from his kingly throne, and they took his glory from him: And he was driven from the sons of men; and his heart was made like the beasts, and his dwelling was with the wild asses: they fed him with grass like oxen, and his body was wet with the dew of heaven; till he knew that the most high God ruled in the kingdom of men, and that he appointeth over it whomsoever he will. Daniel 5:20-21;

And i will say to my soul, Soul, thou hast much goods laid up for many years; take thine ease, eat, drink, and be merry. But God said unto him, Thou fool, this night thy soul shall be required of thee: then whose shall those things be, which thou hast provided? Luke 12:19-20.

Because that, when they knew God, they glorified him not as God, neither were thankful; but became vain in their imaginations, and their foolish heart was darkened, Romans 1:21;

There are not found that returned to give glory to God, save this stranger? Luke 17:18.

In contrast see another Bible figure who understood and acknowldge his source: Paul the Apostle,

"But by the grace of God I am what I am: and his grace which was bestowed upon me was not in vain; but I laboured more abundantly than they all: yet not I, but the grace of God which was with me." 1 Corinthians 15:10.

It is worthy to note that even the savior of the world never arrogated to himself the enablement he manifested.

"Then answered Jesus and said unto them, verily, verily, I say

unto you, The Son can do nothing of himself, but what he seeth the Father do: for what things soever he doeth, these also doeth the Son likewise. I can of mine own self do nothing: as I hear, I judge: and my judgement is just; because I seek not mine own will, but the will of the Father which hath sent me. "John 5:19,30.

There seem to be a quirk in human nature that gives them a false sense of importance in arrogating unto themselves what originally is but a help, gift, grace, favors, anointing, luck etc. This act of refusal to acknowledge his source as coming from God is what YHWH calls pride. Today I decree the dead of every form of pride in our lives, in Jesus name.

* * *

Watch Out

Permit me to share a secret with you today. The devil cannot hurt you but he is smart enough to know and understand that God operates with principles, statutes and precepts. In simple terms, it is called LAWS and COVENANTS. He is also aware of God's love for you, so all of his gimmicks are aimed at getting you to fall out of God's love which actually is your cover. Constantly, he try to get you to break a principle so that whenever God intend sending you enablement, him the devil, the check and accuser master would accuse you before your God, making your blessings to be withheld. See this picture in your Bible:

"But he giveth more grace, wherefore he saith, God resisteth the proud, but giveth grace unto the humble. James 4:6; Surely he scorneth the scorners: but he giveth grace unto the lowly Proverbs 3:34;

Likewise, ye younger, submit yourself unto the elder. Yea, all of you be subject one to another, and be clothed with humility: for God resisteth the proud, and giveth grace to the humble." 1 Peter 5:5.

Please the above should not be misunderstood to mean God as being wicked neither is he monitoring your activities in order to resist or frustrate you rather, understand that his principles, laws and precepts etc. Therefore, it is so in his infinite consistency to act thus when our actions do trigger off either of pride or humility with their attending rewards of either grace or resistance. God is not what the devil is stimulating your experiences, intellect and circumstances to tell you about him. God is who he said he is, which we can only read from his word, the Bible. His consistency and faithfulness to his laws, principles and precepts are infallible therefore, take note that if ever his promises to you be delayed or aborted, either of these two factors could be responsible: direct wickedness or the devil have gotten you to ignorantly bring a principle.

THE GRACE ON NATURE

While science is busy in trying to explain and to give reasons for life and existence, we choose to acknowledge God. Whenever you observe grasses and plantings growing that is a form of grace in display. Whenever you the rains falling, the oceans, rivers and streams flowing, that is grace in display. You constantly are witnessing the grace of God in action whenever you observe a sperm cell in the womb, forming into a fetus then into a human, progressing into a baby who then develops into various stages of growth or anytime someone surrenders his ungodly ways and life to Jesus as Lord and savior and an exchange of salvation of his soul, that is grace. How about that pricking of one's conscience by God's word through a preacher? Consider the coordination of the muscular organ in your mouth called tongue how it mutter sounds distinctive and intelligible, which when interpreted by the brain and understood in various languages, this are all kinds of graces. All of the metabolic activities in your body, how you fall asleep and awake to consciousness is all some kind of grace. How about conception? Is it all mating actions that resulted to pregnancy? Consider the gliding serpent on a rock, can you explain the movement of fishes in waters? Do you posses the secret to wealth creation? Every exploits in discovery by man is just an attempt to comprehend some little formula in order to explain the dimension of God's hidden and wide manifestation of his grace. I could as well say that, skills and abilities are also forms of grace which usually require another kind of grace for results to be obtained. This is why men of skills are not automatic wealth creators. Fruitfulness is but a grace, conception is not an ability to mate, if it were, no man and woman copulating should be barren.

Let's attempt to comprehend man's reason for prolonged answers to prayers resulting from ignorance, partly is centered between the right of ownership and the right of possession and usage. What this implies is that by the grace of God as believers, we have a claim of some rights in Christ Jesus which actually are guaranteed because we have been blessed with all these spiritual blessings in the heavenly places, being a join heir with him in God, but there exists a gulf between our rights of joined claim of ownership and the actual right of possessing those promises for our benefits. This is constantly now under the veils of darkness, and man facing the risk of losing it to the devil's scheming in order to out scheme the Prayerless Christian and to reclaim and possess those promises for our benefits, grace is required to take full delivery of them.

HIS FAITHFULNESS IS BACKING IT.

By no way is God inciting our faith over promises he has no intention to grand for the scripture says far be it from God, that he should do wickedness; and from the almighty that he should commit iniquity..

The Lord is not slack concerning his promises as some men counted slackness; but is longsuffering toward us, not willing that any should perish, but that all should come to repentance. Job 34:10; II Peter 3:9.

Again consider this witness from Hebrews 6:12-18.

That ye be not slothful, but followers of them who through patience inherited the promises. For when God made a promise to Abraham because he could swear by no greater, he swore by himself. Saying, surely blessing I will bless thee, and multiplying I will multiply thee and so, after he had patiently endured, he obtained the promise… wherein God, willing more abundantly to show unto the heirs of promise the immutability of his counsel, confirmed it by an oath. That by two immutable things, in which it was impossible for God to lie...

A close observation from especially the verses from 2Peter above, we could notice the release of grace by God through Jesus Christ; left unutilized by the world for her salvation so we conclude that the gulf between the right of ownership and that of possession is a great display of grace un-utilized; God has played his part of the covenant awaiting man to act his part of the covenant too before salvation can be consummated. Grace is not going to be released, it is already released but until we come to this understanding which in turn bring us to the altar (throne) we could never maximize it. Therefore, the right of ownership, through God's benevolence is freely given, awaiting our claim on the right of possession which we could then apply to our end use.

IT'S A SUBTLE COVENANT.

It has always bothered me on the two opposing axioms in the world the Christians and the secular; the one affirming that "all depends on the grace of God" and the later "man's fate is in his hands". If God by His election of divine providence has selected just a few to engrace, why then should the rest of humanity be judge, having not received what it takes to measure up to standard?

The secular world have more understanding of playing their own part of this covenant hence, they produce more results.

But the supposition of the secular seems to have gained more patronage with attending rewards because, they came closer to understanding the factor that God or nature as being referred to, has done all it's needed to do, so its man's part to decide his fate by pressing further for excellence and genius through knowledge or die a mediocre. This to me, make the secular assume the full responsibility for the attainments while the Christian allow their dogma to hold them down to idleness, inactiveness and mediocrity, supposing God by his grace to dole out to them their expectations, little wonder then, the secular had left the Christians behind. But the Lord commissioned me to raise him priests that will "DO" all that is in his mind, priesthood connotes the highest form of responsibility in all front.

> *"And I will raise me up a faithful priest that shall do according to that which is in mine heart and in my mind, and I will build him a sure house; and he shall walk before mine anointed for-ever... for I have told him that I will judge his house for ever for the iniquity which he knoweth; because his sons made them-selves vile, and he restrained them not, I Samuel 2:35;3:13.*

I am here re-echoing it all over again and shall discuss this respon-sibility as becometh a priest unto our God in details as we pro-ceed further.

IT'S AN ELECTION OF GRACE

And no man taketh this honour unto himself, but he that is called of God, as was Aaron. Hebrews. 5:4.

But ye are a chosen generation, a royal priesthood, an holy nation, a peculiar people; that ye should show forth the praise of Him who hath 'called' you out of darkness into his marvelous light;

Need to say further, it is clear what God is saying in this dispensation. In the Old Testament special few persons were saddled with the responsibility of priesthood but according to the above scripture, all the believers are primarily redeem, called into full responsibility of priesthood.

Deuteronomy 11:18-20 therefore shall 'ye' lay up these my words in your heart and in your soul, and bind them for a sign upon your hand, that they may be as frontlets between your eyes. And ye shall teach them your children, speaking of them when thou sittest in thine house, and when thou walkest by the way, when thou liest down and when thou risest up. And thou shalt write them upon the door posts of thine house, and upon thy gate.

In a close consideration, one will note that the talked about responsibility begins with you the individual, next your family, kindred, community, nation then to the world at large. The unfolding of the whole process of the first tabernacle and the first consecrated priest could all be read in exodus chapter 40:1-38.

Then the LORD said to Moses: "Set up the tabernacle, the Tent of Meeting, on the first day of the first month. Place the ark of the Testimony in it and shield the ark with the curtain. Bring in the table and set out what belongs on it. Then bring in the lampstand and set up its lamps. Place the gold altar of incense in front of the ark of the Testimony and put the curtain at the entrance to the tabernacle. "Place the altar of burnt offering in front of the entrance to the tabernacle, the Tent of Meeting; place the basin between the Tent of Meeting and the altar and put water in it. Set up the courtyard around it and put the curtain at the entrance to the courtyard. "Take the anointing oil and anoint the tabernacle and everything in it; consecrate it and all its furnishings, and it will be holy. Then anoint the altar of burnt offering and all its utensils; consecrate the altar, and it will be most holy. Anoint the basin and its stand and consecrate them. "Bring Aaron and his sons to the entrance to the Tent of Meeting and wash them with water. Then dress Aaron in the sacred garments, anoint him and consecrate him so he may serve me as priest. Bring his sons and dress them in tunics. Anoint them just as you anointed their father, so they may serve me as priests. Their anointing will be to a priesthood that will continue for all generations to come." Moses did everything just as the LORD commanded him. So the tabernacle was set up on the first day of the first month in the second year. When Moses set up the tabernacle, he put the bases in place, erected the frames, inserted the crossbars and set up the posts. Then he spread the tent over the tabernacle and put the covering over the tent, as the LORD commanded him. He took the Testimony and placed it in the ark, attached the poles to the ark and put the atonement cover over it. Then he brought the ark into the tabernacle and hung the shielding curtain and shielded the ark of the Testimony, as the LORD commanded him. Moses placed the table in the Tent of Meeting on the north side of the tabernacle outside the curtain and set out the bread on it before the LORD, as the LORD commanded him. He placed the lampstand in the Tent of Meeting opposite the table on the south side of the tabernacle and set up the lamps before the LORD, as the LORD commanded him. Moses placed the gold altar in the Tent of Meeting in front of the curtain and burned fragrant incense on it, as the LORD commanded him. Then he put up the curtain at the entrance to the tabernacle. He set the altar of burnt offering near the entrance to the tabernacle, the Tent of Meeting, and offered on it burnt offerings and grain offerings, as the LORD commanded him. He placed the basin between the Tent of Meeting and the altar and put water in it for washing, and Moses and Aaron and his sons used it to wash their hands and feet. They washed whenever they entered the Tent of Meeting or approached the altar, as the LORD commanded Moses. Then Moses set up the courtyard around the tabernacle and altar and put up the curtain at the entrance to the courtyard. And so Moses finished the work. Then the cloud covered the Tent of Meeting, and the glory of the LORD filled the tabernacle. Moses could not enter the Tent of Meeting because the cloud had settled upon it, and the glory of the LORD filled the tabernacle. In all the travels of the Israelites, whenever the cloud lifted from above the tabernacle, they would set out; but if the cloud did not lift, they did not set out—until the day it lifted.   So the cloud of the LORD was over the tabernacle by day, and fire was in the cloud by night, in the sight of all the house of Israel during all their travels.

The Spirit of the LORD is by this, calling us to remember that we all are now both Priests and Tabernacles. According to Isaiah 61:6.

"But ye shall be named the priest of the Lord: men shall call you the ministers of our God: ye shall eat the riches of the Gentiles, and in their glory shall ye boast yourselves..."

"Do you not know that your body is the "temple" of the Holy Spirit, who is in you whom you have received from God? You are not your own; don't you know that your-selves are God temple and that Gods spirit lives in you? If any one destroys Gods temple, God will destroy him, for God's temple is sacred, and you are that temple." 1 Corinthians 6:19, 3:16,17.

Since we can't dispute being a temple, likewise should accept that we contain an altar. As you come to him, the living stone- rejected by men but chosen by God and precious to him. You also like living stones, are being built into a spiritual house to be a holy priesthood offering spiritual sacrifices acceptable to God through Jesus Christ 1 Peter 2:4-5.

THE PRIEST

"In his first dealing with the Israelites, any repentant Israelite who had gone through the gate of the tabernacle with his sacrifice and reached the bronze altar had proceeded as far as he dare go along the path of approach to God." In the Old Testament, God appointed mediators between him and man, this they did on behalf of themselves and the people in things pertaining to God upon the altar. It was the responsibility of priests to go on his behalf and carry out spiritual tasks in the Holy place. This they did as representatives for all the people. To them alone was the high privilege of the calling of God to serve him more closely than the congregation of Israel or even then the specially appointed Levites could. This could expressly signify God's intention of having each one of us in a closer relationship with him hence, the splitting of the curtain in the temple upon Jesus' death on the cross.

Before we go further it could be beneficiary for us to look and consider some longtime held views and definitions of this positions, first the universal view;

Secular:

"An authorized minister of a deity who, on behalf of a community, officiates at the altar and in other rites, acting as a mediator between the deity and man."

Let us see that of the Bible.

Spiritual:

A chosen officer or prince with the capacity to draw near to God, for executing the different procedures and ceremonies relating to the worship of God, and for being a representative between God and man" And their duties fell under three main headings (Service, Teaching, and prayer) Something of importance of the priest in Old Testament worship may be judged from the fact that the Hebrew word for priest 'Kohen' occurs almost 800 times. It is interesting that the verb Kahan (from the same root as Kohen) is used in the Old Testament of a bridegroom decking himself with ornaments. It was also their responsibility to wear distinctive clothing whenever they were in attendance at the altar or entered the Holy place their clothing had to be clean and pure before they could approach God. The first mention of a "priesthood" is found in Exodus 19:3-6.....

> *"And Moses went up unto God, and the Lord, called unto him out of the mountain, saying thus shall thou say to the house of Jacob, and tell the children; ye have seen what I did unto the Egyptians, and how I bear you on eagle's wings, and brought you unto myself. Now therefore, if ye will obey my voice indeed, and keep my covenant, then ye shall be a peculiar treasure unto me above all people: for all the earth is mine: and ye shall be unto me a kingdom of priests, and an holy nation. These are the words which thou shall speak unto the children of*

Israel."

IT REQUIRES RESPONSIBILITY FROM YOU!

The grace of God that do not leave you with a responsibility is not a grace to be coveted and it does God no ultimate good in bestowing it. When you consider all that has been discussed, I think grace should be understood as a formular involving instructions of the how, and what, and with a full understanding of the knowledge of God and what is consistent with his nature, requirements and dictates the willingly committed to, and consistently engage on to in order to utilize the released divine enablement from God in accordance to the purpose intended or besoughted for upon the altar of worship.

Maintaining Your Priestly Office:

And one may ask, how do I maintain my office of priesthood? Your office as we have established begins with you, an individual, so we could say you are physically in practice, your home should constitute your primary altar, a physical place of gathering to meet with your God. Next is lightening and keeping the fire burning: this we say is your fervency in the intake of the word, prayer meditation and study. Having lighted up the fire on the altar its of necessity that a sacrifice be laid upon your altar. This is where praise, worship, offering and righteous living comes into place. Because he is attracted to such and he releases grace abundantly upon such as one. Forgiveness, remission and atonement and pardon are herein received with the benefits of his divine voice instructing and guiding us daily. From the above we may rejoin with God that knowledge remain the primary requirement for keeping abreast with this exalted office.

Hosea 4:6,7 "My people are destroyed for lack of knowledge: because thou hast rejected knowledge, I will also reject thee, that thou shall be no 'Priest' to me: seeing thou hast forgotten the law of thy God, I will also forget thy children. As they were increased, so they sinned against me: therefore will I change their glory into shame."

That shall not be your portion. I am emphatic about "the knowledge" not just of any kind, but of Christ Jesus the acceptable priest and your office in your service to God. It is this knowledge that is the yardstick for every priest to ascertain if he or she is still on course and if he is falling out of the way.

❉ ❉ ❉

When the word no longer hold sway in your life and affairs, when your interest is dwindling. The Rhema is getting blurred and your law perishing.

See Ezek.7:24-26.

Wherefore I will bring the worst of the heathen and they shall possess your houses: I will also make the pomp of the strong to cease; and their holy places shall be defiled. Destruction cometh; and they shall seek peace, and there shall be none. Mischief shall come upon mischief, and rumor shall come upon rumor; then shall they seek a vision of the prophet; but the law shall perish from the Priest, and counsel from the ancients.

God is not threatening you and I, rather he is showing to us the way in order to enhance our calling and to discharge our duties in accordance with his patterns, which is Jesus Christ, because in him dwelleth the fullness of Godhead bodily and a typical priest for us to emulate after. The altar in which we are made Priests (Ministers) upon, is Christ. He is our great altar, sacrifice, and Priest. Through his benevolence, we are redeemed to discharge his exemplary office towards God and our provisions are herein reserved for us. In 1Corinthians 9:13; 10:18. We are thus re-assured,

"Don't you realize that those who work in the temple get their meals from the offerings brought to the temple?" and those who serve at the altar get a share of the sacrificial offerings. Think about the people of Israel. Were not they united by eating the sacrifices at the altar?"

Therefore, whenever man is united to the altar, he is privileged to both offer and to partake of the grace upon the altar:

❉ ❉ ❉

Approach to God-sacrifice, atonement, pardon, acceptance, salvation, freedom and protection. All of these men enjoy as benefits while he also offers the sacrifice of his lips, body (righteous living) and materials. So singleness of heart and faith is a mandatory requisite even as we call those things that be not as though they were. Hence, God's word is one of the witnesses on the earth according to Hebrews 10:22; 1John 5:8.

Let us draw near with a true heart in full assurance of faith, having our hearts sprinkled from an evil conscience and our bodies washed with pure water. And there are three that bear witness in earth, The Spirit, and the water, and the Blood: and these three agree in one.

Note, life remains a court room, that means, the more you can proof your case with evidence (The word of God) which you are a witness to, the more chances of winning your cases. God will always be the judge of all, Jesus the Chief advocate while the devil is the accuser.

THRONE:

L et us start by reading some passages to establish what we are about to discuss. Isaiah 6:1-6.

In the year that King Uzziah died I saw also the Lord sitting upon the throne, high and lifted up, and his train filled the temple. Above it stood the Seraphims: each one had six wings; with twain he covered his face, and with twain he covered his feet, and with twain he did fly. And one cried unto another, and said, Holy, Holy, Holy is the Lord of Host: The whole earth is full of his glory. And the posts of the door moved at the voice of him that cried, and the house was filled with smoke. Then said I, woe is me! For I am undone; because I am a man of unclean lips, I dwell in the midst of a people of unclean lips: for mine eyes have seen the King the Lord of Hosts. Then flew one of the Seraphims unto me, having a life coal in his hand which he had taken from off the altar: and he laid it upon my mouth, and said Lo, this hath touched thy lips; and thine iniquity is taken away, and thy sin purged."

There is a throne

"And I saw thrones, and they sat upon them, and judgments was given was given unto them. And I saw a great white throne, and him that sat on it, from whose face the earth and heaven fled away. Thy throne, O God, is forever and ever.... (Revelation 20:4, 11; Psalms 45:6; Hebrews 1:8).

The light shining from the above scriptures which I would like us to see is this: A picture is herein being made clearer alongside its activities upon the throne. We could likewise understand the privilege of being invited unto this throne, obtaining pardon from sin, iniquities and receiving the grace to carry us through in times of need. Also, we are to understand that it was a coal of fire from the same altar that could purge the sins, even the sins of the prophet, and the fire thus signifying the personality and presence of the Holy Spirit. The angels being ministering spirits to the heirs of salvation could thus administer this purging on Isaiah the prophet, the eagle eye prophet. Furthermore, we could see that only after then that the burden of God was unveiled,

"who will go for us?"

Man could thus hear expressly the voice of God his creator distinctively.

According to the dictionary definition: A throne is a ceremonial chair for a sovereign. Though figuratively used here, God is here being equated so to speak in an idiomatic expression by which the object of an office is addressed as a personality and vis-visa the personality being referred to as the office for example: For example, the crown is angry. This referring to a king being displeased.

The potentate of dignity associated with this office, glory, splendor, royalty and magnificence are appalling for a mortal man to approach, yet the sovereign God thus enjoins us to come unto this throne not just timidly intimidated and cowardly but boldly, O my God with confidence of assurance.

"Let us therefore come boldly unto the throne of grace that we may obtain mercy and fine grace to help in time of need." Hebrews

4:16.

Considering the above figurative use of the word throne, along with its definitions one could conclude that a throne is not a ruler but are thus made one by reason of operation and administration. It is in this light of understanding that we shall like to relate further how the throne is also a gate through which access is granted or denied, according to the dictionary, a gate is framed, barrier, usually hinged, used to close an opening made for entrance and exit. God spoke to me on 21st February 2011 that thrones are gates because they either allow or disallow the flow of movement for or against a family, society, community, state or nation and there is no limit to what can flow through this gates, genes, hosting a whole lot of attributes, characteristic, attitude etc, also includes favour, grace wisdom, knowledge wickedness etc. Before we dwell exhaustively on gates let us still look at how a throne could translate into a gate which conversely allows the flow in and out of issues to affect either negatively or positively an individual, community or nation. Herein from the pages of scripture we have a classical example of God giving out some instructions concerning a nation's administrative throne, little did they understand the ensuring consequences of any possible non adherence to such instructions.

"You are about to enter the land the Lord your God is giving you. When you take over and settle there, you may think, We should select a King to rule over us with the nation around us, if this happens, be sure to elect as king the man the Lord your God chooses. You must appoint a fellow Israelite; he may not be a foreigner. The King must not build a large stable of horses for himself or send his people to Egypt to buy horses for the Lord has told you, You must never return to Egypt. "The king must not take many wives for himself, because they will turn his heart away from the Lord. And he must not accumulate large amounts of wealth in silver and gold for himself. When he sits on the throne as King, he must copy for himself this body of instructions on a scroll in the presence of the levitical priests. He must always keep that copy with him and read it daily as long as he lives. That way he will learn to fear the Lord his God by obeying all the terms of these instructions and decrees. This regular reading will prevent him from turning away these commands in the smallest way. And it will ensure that he and his descendants will reign for many generations in Israel Deuteronomy 17:14-20 NLT.

A mere reading of these verses may convey a meaning to be only for the kings' wellbeing and continuity, until we came to the Kings that disobeyed those instructions, only for us to hear God say,

"They caused the children of Israel to sin. 2 Samuel. 24:17, to explain that a King on a throne is also a gate through which certain things could be allowed or disallowed to pass through to either a nation, people or persons.

UNDERSTANDING GATES AS IT RELATES TO THRONES AND ALTARS

Every throne necessarily hosts an altar whether physically expressed and portrayed or implicitly, because homage is paid to thrones and on the throne thus it is empowered mightily with powers of authority to open either way. Permit me to say that the action of every throne is likened to a gate while its base is sited on an altar from which its administrative cord stretches it tentacles.

➢ Gates allow and disallow the flow in and out.

Psalms 24:7-10. Open up, ancient gates! Open up, ancient doors, and let the King of Glory enter. Who is the King of glory? The Lord strong and mighty; the Lord, invisible in battle.

➢ Gate are usually manned by someone.

Jeremiah 37:12-14. Jeremiah started to leave the city on his way to the territory of Benjamin, to claim his share of the property among his relatives there. But as he was walking through the Benjamin gate, a sentry arrested him and said, "You are defecting to the Babylonians!"

➢ The ALTAR is also a gate to the spiritual worlds.

Genesis 28:17. But he was also afraid and said, "What an awesome place is this! It is none other than the house of God, the very gateway to Heaven!" Abraham, his grandfather's place of altar unknown to him.

➢ Every gate usually have an live up to its name.

Esther 4:2. He went as far as the gate of the palace, for no one was allowed to enter the palace gate while wearing cloths of mourning..., Now I say to you are Peter and upon this rock I will build my church, and the gates (The powers of hell) will not conquer it. Matthew 16:18.

➢ Destinies are approved or accused at the gates.

Jeremiah 37:13-16. But as he was walking through the Benjamin gate, a sentry arrested him and said, "You are defecting to the Babylonians!" the sentry making the arrest was Irijah the son of Shelemiah, grandson of Hananiah. "That is not true!" Jeremiah protested. "I had no intention of doing any such thing". But Irijah will not listen, and he took Jeremiah before the officials. They were furious with Jeremiah and had him flogged and imprisoned in the house of Jonathan the secretary... Jeremiah was put into a dungeon cell where he remained for many days.

➢ Destinies are blessed or cursed at the gates.

Palms 9:13. Have mercy upon me, O Lord; consider my troubles which I suffer of them that hate me, thou that liftest me up from the gates of death... after this opened Job his mouth, and cursed his day... Because it shuts not up the doors of my mother's womb, nor hid sorrow from mine eyes. Job 3:1-10; Jere. 20:14

➢ Changes are effected from the gates.

Hebrews 13:12. So also Jesus suffered and died outside the city gate to make his people holy by means of his own blood... Enter his gate with thanksgiving; go into his courts with praise. Psalms 100:4

➢ Gates can be uprooted and planted.

Judges 16:3. But Samson stayed in bed only until midnight. Then he got up. Took hold of the doors of the town gate, including the two posts, and lifted them up, bar and all. He put them on his shoulders and carried them all the way to the top of the hill across from Hebron.

➢ Gates are fashioned, constructed and designed according to purposes.

Psalms 118:19, 20. Open for me the gates where the righteous enter, and I will go in and thank the Lord. These gates lead to the presence of the Lord, and the godly enter there... open the gates to all who are righteous; allow the faithful to enter. Isaiah 26:2; You can enter God's kingdom, only through the narrow gate. The high to hell is broad and its gate is wide for the many who choose that way. Matthew 7:13.

➢ Gates controls "WHAT", "HOW" and "WHEN"

Isaiah 38:10. I said in the cutting off of my days, I shall go to the gates of the grave: I am deprived of the residue of my years.

➢ Gates bear records and witnesses.

Ruth 4:1-11. Boaz went to the town gate and took a seat there. Just then the family redeemer he had mentioned came by... If you will want the land then buy it here in the presence of these witnesses... then the elders and all the people standing in the gate replied, "We are witnesses"!... "As I was in the days of my youth, when the secret of God was upon my tabernacle; when I went out to the gate through the city... it gave witness to me." Job 29:4-11; and he went with his father, Hamor, to present this proposal to the leaders at the town gate. Genesis 34:20.

➢ Gates can be possessed.

Genesis 22:17. That in blessing I will bless thee, and in multiplying I will multiply thy seed as the stars of the heaven, and as the sand which is upon the seashore; and thy seed shall possess the gate of his enemies.

➢ Gates are thrones of authority.

Genesis 19:1. And they came through angel to Sodom at even; and Lot sat in the gate of Sodom... when I went out to the gate through the city, when I prepare my seats in the street! The young men saw me and hid themselves: and the aged arose, and stood up. The princes refrained talking, and laid their hand on their mouth. The nobles held their peace, and their tongue cleaved to the roof of their mouth. Job 29:7-10. See, I have this day set thee over the nations and over the kingdoms, to root out, and to pull down, and to destroy, and to throw down, to build, and to plant... thou art my battle axe and weapons of war: for with thee I will break in pieces the horse and his rider; and with thee I will break in pieces the chariots and his rider Jeremiah 1:10; 51:20-23.

➢ Counsel proceed forth from the gates.

Genesis 34:20-14. And Hamor and Shechem his son came unto the gate of their city, and communed with the men of their city. Saying, these men are peaceable with us: therefore let them dwell in the land, and trade therein, for the land, behold, it is large enough for them, let us take their daughters to us for wives, and let us give them our daughters. Only herein will the men consent unto us for to dwell with us, to be one people, of every male among us to be circumcised as they are circumcised... and every male was circumcised, all that went out of the gate of hid city.

➢ Praise is also a gate.

Isaiah 60:18; 61:11; 62:7... but thou shalt call thy walls salvation, and thy gates praise... so the Lord God will cause righteousness and praise to spring forth before all the nations... and give him no rest, till he establish and till he make Jerusalem a praise in the earth... and it shall be to me a name of joy, a praise and honour before all the nations of the earth Jeremiah 33:9. For I will make you a name and a praise among all the people of the earth Zephaniah 3:20. Praising God, and having favour with all the people. And the Lord added to the church daily such as should be saved. Acts 2:47;

16:25. And at midnight Paul and Silas prayed, and sang praises unto God: and the prisoners heard them... Let the people praise thee, O God; Let all the people praise thee. Then shall the earth yield her increase; and God, even our own God, shall bless us.

➢   Authority and power belongs to those constantly at the gate.   II Kings 3:14; 5:16. And Elisha said, As the Lord of hosts liveth, before whom I stand, surely, were it not that I regard the presence of Jehoshaphat the King of Judah, I will not look toward thee, nor see thee... But he said, As the Lord liveh, before whom I stand, I will receive none... As the Lord God of Israel liveth before whom I stand, there shall not be dew nor rain this years, but according to my word 1 kings 17:1..., For there stood by me this night the angel of God, whose I am, and whom I serve... fear not... be of good cheer: for I believe God, that it shall be even as it was told me. Acts 27:21-25, Genesis 18:1, 22-32. And the Lord appeared unto him (Abraham) in the plains of Mamre: and he sat in the tent door in the heat of the day,... and the men turned their faces from thence, and went toward Sodom: But Abraham stood yet before the Lord... And Moses besought he Lord his God, and said, Lord, why doth thy wrath wax hot against thy people, which thou hast brought forth out of the land of Egypt with great power and with thine mighty hand? Wherefore should the Egyptians speak, and say, for mischief did he bring them out, to slay them in the mountains, and to consume them from the face of the earth? Turn from thy fierce wrath, and repent of this evil against thy people. Remember Abraham, Isaac, and Israel, thy servants, to whom thou swearest by thine own self and saidst unto them, I will multiply your seed as the stars of heaven, and all this land that I have spoken of will I give unto your seed, and they shall inherit it forever. And the Lord repented which he thought to do unto his people.. Exodus 32:11-14.

GRACE IS AVAILABLE, BUT MUST BE ACCESSED.

Herein we see the difference between believers from non believer in the nature of grace made available. Because the laws of God are universal, when a non-believer through knowledge and understanding and a consistency towards the requirements of their desired goals and objectives, do attain their end results by the grace but because they have not met the requirements for being call the children of God therefore no grace is utilized so they can't exhibit his character and nature thereby being unable to please him. But a believer who has met the requirements for being a child of God, grace is then utilized to please God in exhibiting his nature and character but hence he fails to meet the requirements for other endeavours and pursuits, he will lack the grace, not in availability rather in utilization because it is already released to attaining of those aspirations and even his God given visions. Grace is as universal as the air, rain, sun etc of God providences but it universality works within some "terms" and should not be generalized upon every application nor interpretation for example, the air we breathe is some kind of grace yet man plays no part about it other than maximizing it:; its universally free. But the grace for salvation is also universally available but not free, a man's part is required before it can become use full or beneficial. Permit me to quickly answer an interjecting supposition of thought "where in the Bible do God attached a condition to obtaining grace nor grace given on a platform of covenant?" "For grace is free and an un-merited favour". I may as well answer that a woman's conception is a free gift of favour without a husband mating with his wife. Any blessing or promise of God that requires a part of you to act in correspondence to the desired end of such a promise or blessing is automatically a covenant awkwardness, slothfulness lack of zeal, fervency and continuity because we leave all to grace for lack of understanding and when it could not go as anticipated and wrongly expected we fall back. Rather than asking what must I need do in order to fully utilize the released grace for my expectations. See Psalms 44:3. For they got not the land in possession by their own sword, neither did their own arm save them; but thy right hand, and thin arm, and the light of thy countenance, because thou hadst a favour unto them. What are we talking about here? The above verse we read sounds like some guys sat down by the willows playing and making merriment without a sword or any arm nor engaging in any form of a fight but were just whisked by God into possession of a land he has fought and driven out all her inhabitants and disposing them, he handed it over to his children we have failed God enough in our right of possession, I think this is a wakeup call to the church to get understanding and charge forthwith to dispossess and occupy till he comes.

THE INVITATION.

The invitation to come to the throne of grace is God's most important gift to man, come now, let us reason together.... Let us therefore come boldly to the throne of grace. Isaiah 1:8; Hebrews 4:16. He further went on to send his emissaries to extend his invitation by counseling and announcing it. The Lord is with you, while ye be with him; and if ye seek him, he will be found of you; but if ye forsake him, he will forsake you II Chronicles 15:2. Again we see God admonishing us through James. Draw nigh to God, and he will draw nigh to you. James 4:7,8. God's supreme benefit from the invitation stems from his commitment towards restoring man to his lost position (Worshipper-priesthood) as we have been taught that we were created to replace the fallen Lucifer in duty. So man is created to offer to God or better still to covenant with God. What I am advocating is this. They can never be any form of spiritual activities, be it of God with man or the occults with the devil without an altar. An altar remains the only grand meeting grounds on which covenants are enacted, ratified, fortified, promulgate laws, exert desires, influence and authority. An altar is the ground for exchanging of interests, offerings and receiving of benevolences. Man should offer worship to God while God offers grace to man. So when both meet for this exchange of values man become the beneficiary of grace and God the beneficiary of worship and the said meeting point is the altar, be it personal or cooperate the altar remains the only meeting point between man and God. (Spirits)

IT'S A SPIRITUAL PRINCIPLE:

Thoughts precede concepts; idea in its original form gives birth to underlying principle upon which every manifested idea is governed.

Let me attempt to explain some more, the weight of this assertion. The need for this altar became so important that God went on to translate the physical altar to the human heart see what he accomplished in I Peter 2:9,10. But we a chosen generation, a royal priesthood, an holy nation, a peculiar people; that ye should shew forth the praises of him who hath called you out of darkness into his marvelous light which in time past were not a people, but are now the people of God. We can all abound in grace.

God Desires Worship

Now see the deep hunger of need in God. But the hour cometh, now is, when the true worshippers shall worship the father in spirit and in truth: for the father seeketh such to worship him John 4:23.

Worship actually take place in an altar so in the altar, instructions are released and when carried out, grace is utilized to exert on that particular issue. I have under studied a pattern in God and I see it is consistent with his nature and dealing with man that anytime God begins to invite you to an altar a covenant is about to be consummated through exchange of worship and grace (instructions and obedience). See what he said to a people just about to be released from bondage and captivity.

"And he said, certainly I will be with thee, and this shall be a token unto thee, that I have sent thee; when thou hast brought forth the people out of Egypt, ye shall worship God upon this mountain. Exodus 3:12

Maybe if you are thinking and pondering the way I am doing too, then a question could have propped up in your heart now. I am asking the same question too. The question is this "What joy or benefit is there, in being privileged to worship God in a mountain, seeing I am just being released from servitude"? Should not I go all out to celebrate my freedom and deliverance, seeing that I have been denied the privilege for four hundred years? All my life and the life of my forefathers. Should not we be allowed to be free for once to roam, jubilate, make merry and rejoice? For I am no more under task-masters, I have my will, I can do what I feel like now. Perhaps they understood or murmured but I am not certain. I have hoped that they understood because having stayed in Egypt for 430 years, they must have learnt that what empowers a people is the god they worship. Having so many nations before them to journey through and confront, God knows what they need the most, worship a consummation of a covenant on an altar for the release and utilization of grace for advancement. Need I remind you of Balaam and Balak? Through worship he sought to invoke a grace that will out do the Israelite. Thereby over power them. Number 22:23 and 24. Worship and altars have long standing in the history of man that failure to desire to understand and fully comprehend it implications, grace could be so far from such a one. May I admonish you to personally consider this issue of altars seriously in order to draw out the grace you so desire for your life journey. Permit me to flip some pages of the Bible with you as we consider the subject of altars from old to date. But before we proceed shall we try to describe or better still adopt a definition for a better understanding.

THE ALTAR

We have earlier said there can never be any form of spiritual activities be it of God with man or the occults with the devil without an altar. An altar remains the only grand meeting ground upon which covenants are enacted, ratified, fortified, promulgates laws, exert desires, influences and authority enforced. An altar is the ground for exchanging of interests, offerings and receiving of benevolences.

What's An Altar

"An altar is primarily the place of sacrifice; any structure upon which offerings such as sacrifices are made for religious purposes," Altars are usually found at shrines, and can be located in temples (Thrones) churches and other places where worship is received. Altars symbolized a deity in the sacrificial ritual and the victims 'delivered' to the deity by physical contact with the altar. And usually there is a request from worshiper which the altar in turn grant. In order word an altar is a physical medium through which a god is contacted with a worship offered via sacrifices which when accepted, grant benevolence towards a desired end. This act is triggered by the desire for obtaining and securing help and enablement. It's also a landing path for spirits upon invitations when their criteria of demands have been met by humans. An altar is an authorized meeting point of the spirits to legally operate on the material world. The first mention of an altar in scripture is in Genesis 8:20, but note that its not the first altar in existence, "so Noah built an altar to the Lord, and there he sacrificed a burnt offering, the animals and birds that had been approved for that purpose" The above displayed act was not learned in the ark but on old life style practice, though not made reference to nor made mention of, but considering chapter 6:8-9 we clearly see supporting evidences that Noah was already involve in altar worship.

"But Noah found favour with the Lord... Noah was a righteous man, the only blameless person living on earth at the time, and he walked in close fellowship with God."

And it was this Noah, whom later in life along with his son Shem, nutured Abram's young faith in God from age 3 till he was 42 years. Permit me to refer you to some books made mentioned of in the Bible though not canonized amongst the Holy Scriptures, the book of Jasher mention in Joshua 10:12-13 and 2 Samuel 1:8-27. That this books were inferred to means that they contain some facts of information after all, the biblical book of Jude quotes from the book of Enoch in verses 14-15, "Enoch, the seventh from Adam, prophesied about these men: see the Lord is coming……" , also in the same vain, the Apostle Paul quoted Epimenides in Titus 1:12. Contained in the book of Jasher is the accurate account of Abram's birth, early life and faith in God."

A birth party for Abram was opening high drama of the tension and conflict between this newborn and Nimrod, the ruler of Shinar (sumer) During the party an exploding star erupted in the heavens interpreted as an omen of the demise of Nimrod by the hands of Abram. The babe was sent into exile, and eventually to the tutelage of Noah and Shem in Ur Casidim, the land of the Khaldim, or the Ur of the chaldeas the foothill of the Armenian. All the families of shem were inhabiting the Mesopotamian valley after the flood." Abraham's interaction with the altar has been an age – long experience, which born into a family of oracle priests'. The account continues:

"Terah was a worshiper of Marduk, the celestial warrior god, Mars. The tower of Bable was dedicated to this orbiting celestial proto-planet, which returned to an avenging destructive path to earth about every 52-54 years. Imagine the fear, respect and terror created by this protoplanet as every two years it made a commentary pass by over the earth. Each pass by was closer and closer until its nearest and most destructive orbital visit came on a fifty plus years anniversary. An entire governmental department of that early Shiner was devoted to scientific evaluation of this cometary visitor. This department included the conjurors, which developed a whole system of predictive celestial sciences and the magi, wise men, who studied the philosophical, religions, and symbolize was developed to appease Marduk (Mars) and what better than to fashion image in store, or wood and use them in effigies to be placed in their homes for worship. This is the earliest historical depiction of idol worship (Jasher 9:7).

In his urban estate, Terah built twelve large stature which resided in his private temple, constructed of stone and wood. Each effigy represented a deity for the month, representing the calenderer system utilized in Nippur, developed since the Noachian flood and the catastrophe which forced earth to a new and further orbit from the sum of increasing the yearly calendar from 290 to 300 days per years to 360 days per year. The zodiac system was began, and Terah came from a long line of a oracle priests and the first disciples of the Zodiachian secret mysteries. In this book of Jesher, a story is recounted of Arphaxad, who has a son by Rasuja, named Kainian. This Kainan came under the special tutelage of his father and learnt the art of writing. One day on the foothills he uncovered a stone stele with writings which he soon identified as the writing of the watchers, the fallen angels, who wrecked such genetic havoc in the antediluvian world. These writing included the "astrology of the sun and the moon and the stars and in all the signs of heaven" (Jubilee 8:3, compare with book of Enoch 8:1). Kainan hid the writing from the knowledge of Noah but pass the secret mysteries to his son, Kesed and then to his son, Ur the builder of the city of Era of the Chaldeans. It was Ur, who transported this information to the new mystery religion of the Chaldeans and was the first to sculpt molten image for worship. The formation of idol worship was started by Ur, the father of the Chaldeans.

The priestly dynasty passed down through the daughter of Ur, called 'On' who was the mother of Nahor, the grandfather of Abram. The traditions were then passed on to Terah and unto Abram, in his youth he also pondered the meaning of worship, the sun and the moon but came to the thoughtful condition that the creator God was greater than these. In the solitude of the Armenian hillside, the true worship of the creator God and the family traditions in the family of Adam, preserved and transcribed by Noah were given to Abram.

Now having traversed the early life of our patriarch we noticed that altars have always played a significant role in the life of a people in all the sphere of endeavors. It was this influence upon his life and practice that at the mere appearance of God, Abram understood that a deity (God) must have a place of sitting (an Altar) before proper conversation could take place. He dare not leave his God standing without offering him a comfortable throne to sit upon so they could converse.

Geneses 12:7:8 then the LORD appeared to Abram and said, I will give this land to your descendants. "And Abram built an altar there and dedicated it to the LORD, who had appeared to him. After that, Abram traveled south and set up camp in the hill country with Bethel to the west and Ai to the east. There he built another altar and dedicated it to the LORD and he worshiped the LORD... so Abram moved camp to Hebron and settled near the oak grove belonging to Mamre.

There he built another altar to the LORD. When he arrived at the place where God had told him to go, Abraham built an altar and arrange the wood on it. Genesis 13:18; 22:9.

Abraham's dedication, faithfulness and consistency earned him a boast from God, "I know Abraham will teach his children after him to follow me;" little wonder then that Isaac was thus instructed and carefully taught after this practice of altar worship that in Genesis 22:25 we see him living his father's guidance " then Isaac built an altar there and worshiped the Lord; And just as it has become a tradition to pass on this altar worship practices, Isaac, successfully passed it on to Jacob. "And Jacob rose up early in the morning, and took the stone that he had put for his pillows, and set it up for a pillar and poured oil upon the top of it. And he called the name of that place Bethel: And Jacob vowed a vow..." Genesis 28:18-20.

Upon an altar, Jacob renamed a place, expressed his desire and request which were all granted. Again see chapter 33:20; 35:1-7.

"And there he built an altar and named it EL-Elohe- Israel. Then God said to Jacob, "Get ready and move to Bethel and settle there. Built an altar there to the God who appeared to you when you fled from your brother, Esau. "So Jacob told everyone in his household, "Get rid of all your pagan idols, purify yourselves, and put on clean clothing. We are now going to Bethel, where I will build an altar to the God who answered my prayer when I was in distress. He has been with me wherever I have gone." As they set out, a terror from God spread over the people in all the towns of that area, so no one attacked Jacob's family... Jacob built an altar there and named the place El-bethel."

Again note from Moses' action in building of an altar, we conclude that Jacob must have done a good job in passing on to his children the same tradition of his fathers, though for 430 years, no mention of any kind pertaining to an altar was made in the scripture, but surprisingly we see Mosses in Exodus 17:15 building an altar to the Lord "Moses build an altar there and named it Yahweh- nissi (the LORD is my banner) he said. A host of other notable characters in scripture belt and treasured the altar worship, amongst whom are Zerubabel –Ezra 3:2; Samuel- 1Samuel 7:15;17; Joshua-Joshua 8:30; David- II Samuel 24:25. Then you see men like Elijah, whose confidence and boast were in their relationship with the God of their altasr, 1 Kings 17:1.

"And Elijah the Tishbite, who was of the inhabitants of Gilead, said unto Ahab, As the Lord God of Israel liveth before whom I stand, there shall not be dew nor rain these years, but according to my word."

Elisha also in II Kings 3:14: And Elisha said, As the Lord of hosts lived before whom I stand, surely, were it not that I regard the present of Jehoshaphat the king of Judah, I would not look toward thee, nor see thee.... Paul in Acts 27:23. For there stood by me this night the angel of God, whose I am, and whom I serve.

The tenacity of these clutching to an altar, and prioritizing it in their daily life is the height of effectual maximization of the grace received from an altar. Thus one enjoined to an altar become one with the deity of such an altar in authority and power. Having underscored the altar we shall take a closer look also on the significance of this altar to our living. We have already established that the altar afford us a ground for meeting with God but we shall try to find out more that could be benefitted in keeping up with the worship upon an altar. Walter Russell said" you cannot command that which you have not obeyed and you cannot intelligently obey that which you have not understood and to understand, you must seek to be one with him, for our God is a Jealous God who will only whisper to those who have time for him in quietness on the altar of worship. So we see Elijah and Elisha amongst others clearly demonstrate this truth in their life and ministry. In scripture, the first expression connoting an altar and a worshiper is found in Genesis 4 where both Abel and Cain gave offerings to the Lord. Abel sacrifice was pleasing to the Lord but Cain's was not, and instead of seeking the Lord and how to give a pleasing offering upon the altar being a place where God receive or reject sacrifices, he rather got envious and the state of his heart was thus revealed in his offering. It is not pleasing to the Lord. And from the altar, God warns him to do well and be accepted. He warned him that sin lies at the door with a desire to rule over him: vs:6,

"And the Lord said unto Cain, why art thou wroth? And why is thy countenance fallen? If thou doest well, shalt thou not be accepted? And if thou doest not well, sin lieth at the door. And unto thee shall be his desire and, thou shall rule over him."

But he regarded not the warning and murdered his brother. So the first recorded murder was because of an altar. Altars, therefore, have a way of revealing the heart. In Genesis 8, Noah built an altar of thanksgiving to God for keeping him and his family and all the animals safe. And we have this commandment"

"And now, O ye priest, this commandment is for you. If ye will not hear, and if ye will not lay it to heart, to give glory unto my name, saith the Lord of hosts, I will even send a curse upon you, and I will curse your blessings: yea, I have curse them already, because ye do not lay it to heart. Behold, I will corrupt your seed, and spread dung upon your faces, even the dung of your solemn feasts, and one shall take you away with it. And ye shall know that I have sent this commandment unto you, that my covenant might be with Levi saith the Lord of hosts. Malachi 2:1-4.

Servicing of our altars for an onward transmission of grace towards our use is a command, for it keeps pride away and honor God's benevolence towards us all. We can say of Abraham that his was to find and do the will of God, believing God's promises to him.

Genesis 12:8. And he remove from thence unto a mountain on the east of Bathel, and pitched his tent having Bathel on the west, and Ai on the east: And there he builded an altar unto the Lord, and called upon the name of the Lord. Later Abraham return to the place of the altar, to offer sacrifice again. Genesis 13:4 unto the place of the altar, which he had made there at the first: and there Abram called on the name of the Lord. Next we see Abraham build an altar of sacrifice Genesis 22 where God instructed him to offer up his son Isaac as a burnt offering. Abraham obeys even though his son was his only heir, and his birth was a promise and miracle of God. Abraham led his son to mount Moriah and prepared an altar and tied his son upon the altar and as he lifts the knife the angel of the Lord spoke that he should stop- God commends him for his faith and willingness to obey. A ram was found caught in the thicket and offered up instead. Even now we see from these scriptures that altars were important for thanksgiving, and for special sacrifices. They were important enough to be named. They were to remember and tell the experiences to their children. A place for meeting with God, they were made of earth, or unhewn stone. Man did not fashion altar for God. Also we note that, God want us to have a consecrated special place for him. For we are enjoined to draw near to God and he will draw near to us, this becomes necessary to decide on spending time with God as we set aside time to pray and read the scripture and seek him, he fills us with his presence in a fresh way. He gives us wisdom and instructions which when obeyed, grace is obtained. Let me take you back to the day you first came to Christ, it was an altar experience of which you were the sacrifice or offering. You gave your life to God, he gave you righteousness (can you see a covenant there with an exchange taking place?) on the altar God could touch our lives in mighty ways. These could be healing, or miracles, also are times of weeping and repentance. These are times of priestly sacrifice of our lips- praise and worship, just as there are times for petition and intercessions. God is calling you! This is a recovery of priesthood among believers therefore lets endeavor to keep an altar for the Lord- let him LORD over you for once. Our churches must encourage it and give the opportunity to meet with God upon every service. Are we not tired of prayers and counseling sessions in our offices- ministers? Gathering around the altar in prayer and praise as a body of Christ has a sacrifice greater than we could comprehend, there is a dynamic that is supernatural when we pray and praise together. There is a corporate anointing, lives are changed, bondages broken and decisions made for eternity. We see in the life of David that the state of mind to continually yearn for God, his ultimate good, his ways, instructions and a willingness to obey him is prized far better than any sacrifice. And Samuel said,

Hath the Lord as great delight in burnt offering and sacrifices, as in obeying the voice of the Lord? Behold, to obey is better than sacrifice and to hearken than the fat of rams 1Samuel 15:22.

To Cultivate an attitude of seeking, wanting and desiring to be one with him every day through: meditations, prayers and quite-time is a sure way to unite one soul with his creator. This act translates into deep worship, and reverence of his person compelling in us obedience, honor, yieldedness, commitment and trust. At the instance of this, grace is released. I have found out that those who leave in this realm may not necessarily have overcome the everyday sin, but their consciousness having been set towards God, he in turn over looks their short comings. It is demonic and satanic to want to clear your conscience of every sin and wrongs before approaching God. This will amount to self righteousness. Just come, come the way you are and offer him the above and such grace as you have never experienced before would be released to cleans your life. Suffice to say, wake up from your slumber (sin) of any gravity and with a reverence towards God in giving him this worship, oh my Jesus... See what became of this harlot: Luke 7:38, 39:

And, behold, a woman in the city, which was a sinner, when she knew that Jesus sat at meat in the Pharisee's house, brought an alabaster box of ointment, and stood at his feet behind him weeping, and began to wash his feet with tears, and did wipe them with the hairs of her head, and kissed his feet, and anointed them with the ointment. Now when the Pharisee which had bidden him saw it, he spake within himself, saying, This man, if he were a prophet, would have known who and what manner of woman this is that touched him: for she is a sinner.

Did you see any confession?

Consider David during his error in numbering Israel.

2 Samuel 24:24, 25: And the king said unto Araunah, Nay; but I will surely buy it of thee at a price: neither will I offer burnt offer-

ings unto the Lord my God of that which doth cost me nothing. So David bought the threshing floor and the oxen for fifty shekels of silver. And David built there an altar unto the Lord, and offered burnt offerings and peace offerings. So the Lord was entreated for the land, and the plague was stayed from Israel.

Did you see any confession?

Come out from those condemnation! You are a parent: when you return home and your children are playing or eating. Do they wash their hands before rushing towards you? Or do you ignore them to first go and wash their hands? Why would you equate the greatest purifier to turn you back to first go wash your hands? Do any other better place to wash exist other than him? Your Jumping into his pool will never muddy his waters no matter your filthiness. Come unto him, worship and bow unto our God in reverence. Oh Jesus. In sighting your father, you don't run aimlessly away, you run towards his direction. There is a direction to run towards to: it is called throne. This grace reserved by our Lord, though he has brought it, must be properly understood. There is a grace, and an invitation is sent out to inform and invite us:

Hebrews 4:16. Let us therefore come boldly unto the throne of grace that we may obtain mercy and find grace to help in time of need.

GRACE HAS A CUSTODIAN

This grace is in custody and the custodian dwells on a throne. Now let's see how to approach this throne. The Psalmist gave us a lee way herein from his own personal experiences: Enter into his gates with thanksgiving, and into his courts with praise:- Psalms 100:4. In your quest for obtaining this grace, your journey commences from his gate and your success or failure begins and end from this start point. Until access is granted, weeping must continue to trail its denials. This point of the gate is so crucial because, it is herein empowered to either allow or disallow access. It is to be considered such an exposition from the Psalmist who has provided us with a guide on how to have access granted to us. Some might ask why must I begin or enter his gates with thanksgiving for what am not sure nor obtained yet? Historically, from the ancient times it has always been considered an evil conspiracy in the heart of anyone who appears before a king with a sad countenance which in most cases attracted a death sentence according to the rules of the court. Note: it is a rule-Principle. You don't start by breaking a court's principle yet implore same to grant your petitions. Needless to say, that it should be considered a privilege for there was no coming into the king's presence uncalled: All the king's servants and the people of the king's provinces, do know, that whosoever, whether man or woman, shall come unto the king into the inner court, who is not called, there is but one law of his to put him to death, except such to whom the king shall hold out the golden sceptre, that he may live: but I have not been called to come in unto the king these thirty days: Esther

4:11. And it came to pass in the month Nisan, in the twentieth year of Artaxerxes the king that wine was before him: and I took up the wine, and gave it unto the king. Now I had not been beforetime sad in his presence. Wherefore the king said unto me, why is thy countenance sad, seeing thou art not sick? This is nothing else but sorrow of heart. Then I was very sore afraid: Nehemiah 2:2. It's now clear that every coming into the king's presence should be considered with utmost privilege and the rules strictly adhered to in order to have a fruitful appearance with the throne without risking your very lives. For the KING of kings has aforetime warned the Israelites not to breach his presence lest he fell upon such a person:

Exodus 19:11-13, 21-25 Be sure they are ready on the third day, for on that day the Lord will come down on Mount Sinai as all the people watch. Mark off a boundary all around the mountain. Warn the people, 'Be careful! Do not go up on the mountain or even touch its boundaries. Anyone who touches the mountain will certainly be put to death. No hand may touch the person or animal that crosses the boundary; instead, stone them or shoot them with arrows. They must be put to death.' However, when the ram's horn sounds a long blast, then the people may go up on the mountain." Then the Lord told Moses, "Go back down and warn the people not to break through the boundaries to see the Lord, or they will die. Even the priests who regularly come near to the Lord must purify themselves so that the Lord does not break out and destroy them." "But Lord," Moses protested, "the people cannot come up to Mount Sinai. You already warned us. You told me, 'Mark off a boundary all around the mountain to set it apart as holy.'" But the Lord said, "Go down and bring Aaron back up with you. In the meantime, do not let the priests or the people break through to approach the Lord, or he will break out and destroy them." So Moses went down to the people and told them what the Lord had said. Unfortunately, humans attempting to break God's principle instructed left them with the undesirable of his inexorable and inherent consequences. The camp will be ready to move when Aaron and his sons have finished covering the sanctuary and all the sacred articles. The Kohathites will come and carry these things to the next destination. But they must not touch the sacred objects, or they will die. So these are the things from the Tabernacle that the Kohathites must carry.

His express warnings above yet didn't deter man from violating until he was compelled to uphold the integrity of his infallible word; Uzzah became a victim:

2 Samuel 6:5-7. David and all the people of Israel were celebrating before the Lord, singing songs and playing all kinds of musical instruments—lyres, harps, tambourines, castanets, and cymbals. But when they arrived at the threshing floor of Nacon, the oxen stumbled, and Uzzah reached out his hand and steadied the Ark of God. 7 Then the Lord's anger was aroused against Uzzah, and God struck him dead because of this. So Uzzah died right there beside the Ark of God.

My dear, God holds dear to his integrity of preserving and upholding his word and holiness which we should thus draw near in reverence and appropriate preparations. But thanks be to our Lord Jesus whom through his death and resurrection, we are no longer limited but now have access to the KING of kings at all times to the throne of grace we come as we are. Therefore, it was proper with God to communicate unto us the acceptable pattern while establishing the first tabernacle in the wilderness and the whole chapter of Exodus 25 is explaining the pattern and the last verse went on to admonish Moses to ensure that the pattern is followed through, verse 40...

The LORD said to Moses, "Tell the Israelites to bring me an offering. You are to receive the offering for me from each man whose heart prompts him to give. These are the offerings you are to receive from them: gold, silver and bronze;   blue, purple and scarlet yarn and fine linen; goat hair; ram skins dyed red and hides of sea cows; acacia wood;   olive oil for the light; spices for the anointing oil and for the fragrant incense; and onyx stones and other gems to be mounted on the ephod and breastpiece. "Then have them make a sanctuary for me, and I will dwell among them.   Make this tabernacle and all its furnishings exactly like the pattern I will show you. "Have them make a chest of acacia wood—two and a half cubits long, a cubit and a half wide, and a cubit and a half high. Overlay it with pure gold, both inside and out, and make a gold molding around it.   Cast four gold rings for it and fasten them to its four feet, with two rings on one side and two rings on the other.   Then make poles of acacia wood and overlay them with gold.   Insert the poles into the rings on the sides of the chest to carry it. The poles are to remain in the rings of this ark; they are not to be removed. Then put in the ark the Testimony, which I will give you.   "Make an atonement cover of pure gold—two and a half cubits long and a cubit and a half wide. And make two cherubim out of hammered gold at the ends of the cover.   Make one cherub on one end and the second cherub on the other; make the cherubim of one piece with the cover, at the two ends. The cherubim are to have their wings spread upward, overshadowing the cover with them. The cherubim are to face each other, looking toward the cover.   Place the cover on top of the ark and put in the ark the Testimony, which I will give you. There, above the cover between the two cherubim that are over the ark of the Testimony, I will meet with you and give you all my commands for the Israelites. "Make a table of acacia wood—two cubits long, a cubit wide and a cubit and a half high. Overlay it with pure gold and make a gold molding around it. Also make around it a rim a handbreadth wide and put a gold molding on the rim.   Make four gold rings for the table and fasten them to the four corners, where the four legs are. The rings are to be close to the rim to hold the poles used in carrying the table. Make the poles of acacia wood, overlay them with gold and carry the table with them. And make its plates and dishes of pure gold, as well as its pitchers and bowls for the pouring out of offerings. Put the bread of the Presence on this table to be before me at all times. "Make a lampstand of pure gold and hammer it out, base and shaft; its flowerlike cups, buds and blossoms shall be of one piece with it. Six branches are to extend from the sides of the lampstand—three on one side and three on the other. Three cups shaped like almond flowers with buds and blossoms are to be on one branch, three on the next branch, and the same for all six branches extending from the lampstand. And on the lampstand there are to be four cups shaped like almond flowers with buds and blossoms. One bud shall be under the first pair of branches extending from the lampstand, a second bud under the second pair, and a third bud under the third pair—six branches in all. The buds and branches shall all be of one piece with the lampstand, hammered out of pure gold. "Then make its seven lamps and set them up on it so that they light the space in front of it. Its wick trimmers and trays are to be of pure gold. A talent of pure gold is to be used for the lampstand and all these accessories. See that you make them according to the pattern shown you on the mountain.

Now of the things which we have spoken this is the sum:- We have such an high priest, who is set on the right hand of the throne of the majesty in the heavens: A minister of the sanctuary, and of the true tabernacle, which the Lord pitched, and not man. For every high priest is ordained to offer gifts and sacrifices: where fore it is of necessity that this man has somewhat also to offer. For if he were on earth, he should not be a priest, seeing that there are priests that offer gifts according to the law: who serve unto the example and shadow of heavenly things, as Moses was admonished of God when he was about to make the tabernacle: for, see, saith he, that though make all things according to the pattern showed to thee in the mount. Hebrews 8:1-5... And the man said unto me, Son of man, behold with thine eyes, and hear with thine ears, and set thine heart upon all that I shall shew thee; for to the intent that I might shew them unto thee art thou brought hither: declare all that thou seest to the house of Israel. Ezekiel 40:4... And the LORD said unto me, Son of man, mark well, and behold with thine eyes, and hear with thine ears all that I say unto thee concerning all the ordinances of the house of the LORD, and all the laws thereof; and mark well the entering in of the house, with every going forth of the sanctuary. Ezekiel 44:5.

A careful study of the above passages, reveals that a pattern is consistent with God in accessing him, when we shall delight ourselves in God to offer him our best of adoration and worship, a pattern of faithfulness is being cultivated. Enthroning him over our lives and desiring his Lordship over our choices. A mind not yet complacent (positive) to God can't submit to the laid down pattern. Access to the throne must be soughed for with a consistency of faithfulness as becoming depending of him entirely only then would you begin to grapes and appreciate the pattern for approaching him. For, if not for the already established relationship between a child with his father, how then should such a child dare to run towards him. A relationship of worship will guarantee at any time an access unto the throne. A functional relationship with an understanding ensures a level of trust in the heart of a child enabling him to cast his care and burden while trusting and relying on the father's providences, this is another form of worship. God in his infinite wisdom designed life to be eased and engraced for smooth operation but contrary would be the case when it's lacking.

And Wisdom and Knowledge shall be the stability of thy times, and strength of salvation: the fear of the Lord is his treasure.1 saiah 33:6.

God desires you to become stable in the pattern of worship that will ensure grace upon you and to achieve that, you need an understanding of the entire operational system. He said you need wisdom (application software) and Knowledge (operational software).

God cried out pain of how his own people are being destroyed, toiling hard, experiencing disfavor and loses etc.

My people are destroyed for lack of Knowledge: because thou hast rejected knowledge, I will also reject thee, that thou shalt be no priest to me: seeing thou hast forgotten the law of thy God, I will also forget thy children. Hosea 4:6.

I don't know what your belief is but if you are redeemed you were brought into priesthood (1 Peter 2:9) and only knowledge can sustain you in this office in all of your dealings with Jehovah. Destruction and perishing is not an absent of grace rather its ignorance of it (lack of knowledge) denying you access and application. Consider again:

For it is a people of no understanding: therefore he that made them will not have mercy on them, and he that formed them will shew them no favour. Isaiah 27:11.

The grace that will deliver help to us can be denied on the account of the lack of understanding of its concept. Just like failure to the understanding of salvation is not God's wickedness to punish anyone but the person's ignorance rubbing him of help. Grace is meant to give help in times of need, that particular time of need is called the set time. There is a set time to favour Zion only when Zion understands its operations and if by grace, then is it no more works: otherwise grace is no more. Roman 11:6.

Good understanding giveth favour: but the way of transgressors is hard. Proverbs 13:15.

Grace for help is delivered on a covenant term of understanding or your ways remains hard. For whoso findeth me findeth life, and shall obtain favour of the Lord. Proverbs 8:35. This is wisdom talking and you better listen to her because only she can stabilize you. Isaiah 33:6. Else you may be in the church and still complain because the pattern for obtaining it is ignored.

Turn you at my reproof behold, I will pour out my spirit (grace) unto you, I will make known my words unto you. Because I have called, and ye refused; I have stretched out my hand, and no man regarded; but ye have set at nought all my counsel, and would none of my reproof: I also will laugh at your calamity; I will mock when your fear cometh; when your fear cometh as desolation, and your destruction and anguish cometh upon you. They shall they call upon me, but I will not answer; they shall seek me early, but they shall not find me: for that they hated knowledge, and did not choose the fear (reverence) of the Lord; they would none of my counsel they despised all my reproof. Therefore shall they eat of the fruit of their own way, and be filled with their own devices. For the turning away of the simple shall slay them, and the prosperity of fools shall destroy them. But whoso heakeneth unto me shall dwell safely, and shall be quiet from fear of evil. Proverbs 1:23-33.

Therefore, as ye abound in everything in faith, and utterance, and knowledge, and in all diligence, and in your love to us, see that ye abound in this grace also. II Corinthians 8:7. "Behold, I have taught you statutes and judgments,

(a law passed by a parliament council etc and formally written down. A formal RULE of an institution or organization. A described and layed down pros and cons by this Rule of law which can be punishable for non-adherence to) (this also includes precepts: a formal rule on which a way of THINKING or BEHAVING is based)

even as the Lord my God commanded me, that ye should do so in the land whither ye go to possess it. Keep therefore and do them; for this is your wisdom and your understanding in the sight of the nations, which shall hear all these statutes, and say, surely this great nation is a wise and understanding people. Therefore, abounding in grace is not a prayer topic, nor an event but a realm (a way of life) to be lived in. It is designed by God and those who think and behave according to this realm, God called them Priests. According to 1 Peter 2:9,10. It is a new status in life to walk above the perils of this world, engraced to operate with ease Isaiah 27:11. A good understanding of it will deliver results without hardship. Proverbs. 13:15. And when you continue in thinking and behaving in complacent to delighting in God, you become surrounded by such a dimension of its aroma that compels acceptability Ephesians 1:6 strikes awe and wonder among the nations, Deuteronomy 4:15,6. You grow above criticism to praise – worthiness, the general perception about you changes Galatians 2:9. Your language get changed and seasoned, even as his word resides in your heart. Colossians 3:16.

ACKNOWLEDGEMENT

I would like to acknowledge the foremost spiritual guardian and hedge God by his own election brought and placed over me, Bishop Dr. David O. Oyedepo whom through many visionary encounters I am fashioned. Dr. Paul Enenche also, whom by the Lord, through visions and sitting under his ministrations more lights and understanding had come, giving me directions and revelational visions of my future. Also, Prophet Denis Mongba whom the Lord used to announce and introduce the season for my literary work; he by prophetic word mentioned this book's title, without any idea about its existence in my shelf and same week, the door was opened for me to do a Master's program on e-Book Creation & Publishing with Amazon.com which upon graduating, I am graduated from being a writer to a Publisher. And most dearly is the wonderful partner: Asogwa Chidinma, who from the first day bought into this vision and by whom God have used to bring to fruition the gradual revealing glory of my destiny through her encouragements, the registration of this organisation, being there, my parallel communication partner, you have been a healing and a sun to my heart. This project became a reality through your faith, commitment and belief in me and the vision which has made me a self-published author, starting internationally and from the cloud as it was revealed unto me of the Lord. Most lovely, are Kohen Akpeh-Osowo (KAV) and Chokhmah Agbenu VynEdison (CAV), you loaned out daddy during this long period of wilderness experience. And to all who encouraged and supported me all through this periods especially my big Aunts: Mrs Kenny Okorie, Mrs. Obi Bisong, Mrs. Corona Ushie: my dearest Egogo Eunice Iyombe you have been wonderful and Mr. Ifidon Dominic, you've been a family and to you all that I couldn't mention your names, I appreciate you.

ABOUT THE AUTHOR

Ogar A. Vynedison

Ogar A. VynEdison, Apostle. Is a Consultant, Trainer, Teacher, Publisher also the author of Practical Guide to e-Book Creation & Publishing. Apostle Edi, as fondly called holds various certifications from the following: Shelter Ministerial Academy, School of Christian Counselling, Ministry of the Bible Leaque USA, and Leadership certificate from the Word of Faith Bible Institute. Most recently, a Masters on e-Book Creation and Publishing from {WRITE-FOR-ME}, Amazon.com USA. He holds a certificate also in Renewable Energy, Diploma in Computer Graphics, and a certificate in Creative Arts & Designs. Current he is the CEO of Radah Int'l Systems, an organization which provides: Educational training, Empowerment & Consultancy, focused on the Youth's Rescue of Identity, Dominion & Leadership. CEO, Youth Discovery & Identity magazine and Visioneer: Priests'Kingdom Tabernacle Worldwide, based in Abuja, Nigeria. Hobbies: Drawing & Painting, Driving, Traveling, Cooking, Relating with Children/youth, Teaching, Reading/Writing & Meditation.